MW00414359

OUTPOURING OF THE SOUL

Hishtap'kuth HaNefesh

OUTPOURING OF THE SOUL

Rabbi Nachman's Path in Meditation

Translated from:
Hishtap'khuth HaNefesh

with an introduction and notes
by
Rabbi Areyh Kaplan

Published by
The Breslov Research Institute

ISBN 0-930213-14-9

for further information:
Breslov Research Institute
PO Box 5370
Jerusalem, Israel
or:
Breslov Research Institute
POB 587
Monsey, NY 10952-0587
USA

cover design: Ben Gasner

This book
is dedicated to

Akiva Betzalel Gavriel
& Frimet Ziporah
Hannan

and to their children

Michael Moshe
Avigail Eden
Galah Rachel
Reuven Israel
Ashera Michal

PUBLISHER'S PREFACE

The prophet Jeremiah said, "Rise, cry out at night, at the beginning of the watches, *pour out your heart* like water before God; lift your hands up to Him for the lives of your youth, who faint from hunger on every street" (Lamentations 2:19).

The Midrash[1] teaches that God sent ten harsh famines to the world. Of these, nine occurred during Biblical times. The tenth famine, however, occurs in each generation. It is the hunger described by the prophet as, "a hunger, not for bread, a thirst, not for water, but to hear the word of God" (Amos 8:11).

The Talmud[2] teaches that only prophecies that were said for all generations were recorded; those which did not have a universal message was not preserved in the Bible. Therefore, Jeremiah's words must have a significance for all generations.

Jeremiah lived during the destruction of the first Temple. He *saw* the Israelite children fainting in the streets from hunger, begging and pleading for sustenance. But he also foresaw the Israelite children seeking, searching, and even begging, for their spiritual sustenance during the long years of the exile. His advice was, "Arise, cry out! *Pour out your heart* and soul in prayer before God. This is the only path to true salvation.

Rabbi Alter of Teplik, one of the leading Breslover chassidim in Europe at the turn of the century, saw a similar hunger in his time. He therefore gathered all the writings of Rabbi Nachman and his disciple, Rabbi Nathan of Nemerov, that dealt with meditation (*hithbodeduth*) and published them in a single book. He called this book *Hishtapchuth HaNefesh* ("Outpouring of the Soul").

---

1. *Bereshith Rabbah* 25:3.
2. *Megillah* 14a.

In our time, if anything, this hunger is stronger still. Many Jewish youth are exploring meditation, often in the form of Eastern religions, or, worse still, in the various cults. Many have searched the world, hoping to find a spiritual uplifting. We are experiencing the worst pangs of the famine described by the Midrash, where one must search for the word of God. But here too, Jeremiah's advice stands strong: "Pour out your heart before God."

Yeshivat Chasidei Breslov of Jerusalem would like to express its warmest and heartfelt thanks to Rabbi Aryeh Kaplan, whose initiative led to the translating and publication of this most important work of Rabbi Nachman. We are currently planning to translate and publish other works of Rabbi Nachman, which we hope will be available in the near future.

Chaim Kramer
Menachem Av, 5740

CONTENTS

CONTENTS

The Hebrew word for meditation is *hithbodeduth* (התבודדות).The word occurs in this context in Judaic writings spanning over a thousand years, and is used for all the various forms of Jewish meditation. Yet, in most people's minds, it is primarily with Rabbi Nachman of Breslov (1772-1810) that this word is associated.

Many types of meditation were used by Jewish saints and mystics. A vast wealth of ancient literature describes how the prophets of Israel used meditation to reach their high spiritual states.[1] Similar methods were probably used in Talmudic times. They involved repeating a divine name many times to induce the meditative state.[2]

Other schools made use of the meditative techniques found in the *Book of Creation (Sefer Yetzirah)*. These meditative methods made use of the letters of God's name, accompanied by controlled breathing and specified head motions.[3] However, as the masters of these schools themselves warned, these were extremely powerful and dangerous methods.

The publication of the Zohar opened the path to another meditative method involving Unifications (*Yechudim*). This involved contemplating divine names, and manipulating their letters. These were meditations that, besides inducing a mystical state, would help unify and integrate the personality. The method of *Yichudim* was particularly favored by the Safed school of Kabbalah, and it forms the basis of the mysticism of the Ari (Rabbi Yitzchak Luria, 1534-1572). However, these meditations were not for the average person either; without proper preparation, they could severely damage the mind.

---

1. This, along with Jewish meditation in general, is discussed at length in my book, *Meditation and the Bible*.
2. As described in *Hekhaloth Rabathai* 16.
3. See *Pardes Rimonim* 21.1.

An ancient method of meditation involved the formal prayers. One of the Baal Shem Tov's most important accomplishments was to use the prayers as a safe method of meditation, which could be done by even the simplest person. The way of prayer, as taught by the Baal Shem Tov, involved nothing more than the regular prayer service, said three times daily by every Jew.

The focal point of the prayer service is the *Amidah* or *Shemonah Esreh*, a collection of eighteen (or actually, nineteen) blessings, which is repeated three times each day. This prayer was composed by the Great Assembly just before the close of the prophetic period. There is considerable discussion as to why a single prayer was prescribed to be repeated over and over each day. However, there is considerable evidence that the entire *Amidah* was meant to be used as a meditative device.

After a person has repeated the *Amidah* every day for a few years, he knows the words so well that they become an integral part of his being. It does not take any real mental effort on his part to recite the words, and thus, it is very much like repeating a single word or phrase over and over. If a person clears his mind of all other thoughts, and concentrates on the words of the *Amidah*, this prayer can induce an extremely high meditative state. This is borne out in practice. The same is true of the other parts of the service that are recited daily.

The Talmud notes that the Early Saints (*Chasidim Rishonim*) would spend an hour reciting the *Amidah*.[4] Since the *Amidah* contains some 500 words, it comes out that they would have been reciting one word approximately every seven seconds. It is proven by experience that reciting even the first section of the *Amidah* at such a pace will induce a high meditative state.

---

4. *Berakhoth* 32b. See *Cheredim, Teshuvah* 3.

In an important teaching, the Talmud states, "One who prays must direct his eyes downward and his heart on high."[5] One of the important commentators, Rabbi Yonah Gerondi (1196–1263) explains, "This means that in one's heart, he should imagine that he is standing in heaven. He must banish all worldly delights and bodily enjoyments from his heart. The early sages taught that if one wishes to have true concentration (*kavanah*), he must divest his body from his soul."[6]

A few decades later, this was expressed even more explicitly by the great codifier, Rabbi Yaakov ben Asher (1270–1343) in his *Tur*. Speaking of "saints and men of deed," he writes, "they would meditate (*hithboded*) and concentrate in their prayers until they reached a level where they would be divested of the physical. The transcendental spirit would be strengthened in them until they would reach a level close to that of prophecy."[7] This passage is quoted verbatim by Rabbi Yosef Caro (1488–1575) in his *Shulchan Arukh*, the standard code of Jewish law.[8]

The idea of using the prayer service as a meditative device thus did not originate with the Baal Shem Tov. But the Baal Shem Tov taught the way of prayer as a method that could be used by anyone, from the greatest Kabbalist to the simplest individual. Rather than concentrate on Kabbalistic concepts, a person would focus his entire mind on the words of the prayer, making them fill his entire consciousness. He would then rise from one level to the next, until he was in a deep meditative state.

Although this method was extremely effective and widespread, it was still difficult for many people. Since the formal prayers were said daily, it required a high degree of concentration to avoid allowing one's mind to wander and to

---

5. *Yevamoth* 105b.
6. Commentary on Rif, *Berakhoth* 22b. Also see Ramban on Leviticus 18:4; *Nefesh HaChaim* 2:14 in note.
7. *Tur, Orach Chaim* 98.
8. *Orach Chaim* 98:1. Also see *Toledoth Yaakov Yosef, Acharey*, (Koretz 1780) p. 88c.

keep one's thoughts focused on the words. As Rabbi
Nachman puts it, since the formal prayers are a well traveled
path, there are many destructive forces that lie waiting along
it, ready to trap the unwary.

A great-grandson of the Baal Shem Tov, Rabbi
Nachman extended the way of prayer to make it more
universal and effective. He taught the importance of reciting
the Psalms and other non-obligatory prayers to prepare
oneself for deep meditation. The individual was to banish all
thoughts from his mind, so that he would be completely alone
with God. The next stage would be to banish the ego, so that
all his awareness would be focused on nothing but God.

Most of the methods that had been used were externally
directed, structured meditations. They depended on
predetermined words or images, which constituted a
meditative focus outside the mind. While they were effective
for many people, the very fact that they were externally
directed meant that they were not specifically geared to each
person's needs.

There is another basic method of meditation that is
internally directed. Classically, this consists of meditating on
thoughts, feelings or mental images that arise spontaneously
in the mind. Usually, this is best accomplished by focusing on
a general idea, around which these thoughts will be evoked.
Since there is no formal or predetermined method of evoking
such thoughts, this is most commonly an unstructured
meditation.

Internally directed meditation can be practiced solely in
thought, or, as in some systems, one's thoughts can also be
verbalized. One of the best methods of verbalizing such
thoughts while keeping them concentrated on a single focus
is to express them as spontaneous prayer. This method was to
form the basis of the meditative system of Rabbi Nachman.

The tradition of spontaneous prayer has a long history in
Judaism and was quite prevalent in Biblical and Talmudic
times. Besides the formal services, Jews would always pray to
God in their own language and in their own words, asking

Him for their needs. A constant prayer was that God should draw the supplicant close to Him, and help him attain a closeness to the Divine.

The line between such prayer and meditation is often very blurry. It is obviously possible to pray in one's words without entering a meditative state. Many people offer spontaneous prayers while in a normal, mundane state of consciousness. However, if one recites such prayers slowly and quietly, banishing all thoughts but those of the Divine, such prayer can bring a person into a deep meditative state.

Rabbi Nachman realized that such "conversations with God" were not always easy. For one thing, such a conversation requires a high degree of spiritual commitment. For another, a person initially confronted with the Divine, may easily be at a loss for words. Rabbi Nachman speaks of this "bashfulness" and discusses means with which it can be overcome.

Rabbi Nachman was aware of structured meditations, but he saw them primarily as a means of preparation for the internally directed method. Thus, he taught that if one could not find anything to say to God, he should merely take a word, and repeat it over and over during his meditative period each day. This same word could be repeated for weeks and months, until one found the right words with which to speak to God.

For those familiar with Eastern mantra meditation, this method may seem familiar. A particular phrase that Rabbi Nachman taught could be repeated was "Lord of the Universe," *Ribono Shel Olam* (רבונו של עולם) in Hebrew. A "mantra" such as this, used over a long period, could be the gateway to deeper forms of meditation.

In order to clear the mind for meditation, Rabbi Nachman prescribed the silent scream. Many relaxation methods for the body involve the voluntary tensing of the muscles, and then a determined relaxation of each one. In a way, the silent scream is a voluntary tensing of the mind, which can then be followed by determined relaxation in meditation. It is an extremely effective method for initiating the meditative state.

Another meditative method taught by Rabbi Nachman involved speaking to various parts of the body. In Breslov tradition, this is seen as an important method of self-improvement. Thus, if one wishes to learn to control his tongue, he can speak to it, and literally tell it to practice self-control. The same is true of all other parts of the body. With this method, a person can learn to gain complete and absolute self-control. Here too, one does not merely speak to the part of the body; he does so while in a meditative state.

There are some who might confuse this with autosuggestion or self-hypnosis. However, many psychological and physiological studies have indicated major differences between the hypnotic and the meditative state. Where hypnotism often alters or blocks out awareness, the ultimate goal of meditation is to increase and expand awareness. Where the hypnotic state is usually a state of constricted consciousness, the meditative state is seen as a state of expanded consciousness.

Although *hithbodeduth* denotes meditation, as Rabbi Nachman saw it, it was also a form of personal prayer. Indeed, this is how most contemporary Breslover Chasidim see it. It is seen not so much as a means to attain higher states of consciousness, but as a path toward self-perfection. If a person is constantly conversing with God, he is certain to become more Godly. When he develops a strong bond with God, he is sure to have a greater desire to do God's will.

Beyond that, consistent personal prayer is seen as a means to a good life, even here on earth. When a person discusses his problems with a friend, they no longer seem so formidable. If one can truly learn to discuss them with God, they virtually shrink into insignificance. As one Breslover Chasid put it, "When you bring your problems to God, they cease to exist. There is nothing in the world to worry about." Or, as King David expressed it almost three millenia ago,

"Place your burden on God, and He will carry (it for) you"
(Psalms 55:23).

Rabbi Nachman's major teachings regarding meditation
were collected in a small book, known as *Hishtap'khuth
HaNefesh* (השתפכות הנפש), literally, "Outpouring of the
Soul." The book was rewritten by Rabbi Moshe Yehoshua
Bezishianski, better known as Reb Alter of Teplik, and first
published in Jerusalem around 1904. Reprinted numerous
times, the book is the classic exposition of Rabbi Nachman's
system of meditation and prayer.

When the book was first published, the concept of
meditation had virtually been forgotten in Jewish circles.
However, with increased general interest ·in meditation,
many ancient Jewish sources that discuss the subject have
been rediscovered and studied with renewed interest. In this
context, the *Hishtap'khuth HaNefesh* fits perfectly. It
provides a path through which even the most unlearned Jew
can find his way back to God.

Aryeh Kaplan
18 Tammuz, 5780

AUTHOR'S INTRODUCTION

AUTHOR'S INTRODUCTION

Who is the person who desires life?[1] Who is truly concerned about himself? Who is the one who wishes to be worthy of serving God through prayer, which is a person's main source of life, as it is written, "Prayer to God is my life" (Psalms 42:9). Through prayer, one can also bring life-force to all the spiritual universes.[2]

Let such a person pay close attention to the lessons gathered in this book, which speaks of the importance of prayer and meditation, especially regarding "pouring out one's soul and heart like water before God's presence."[3] He will learn how to ask God for all that he needs, both materially and spiritually. This is the only way that one can receive divine help at all times.

This holy path is an ancient one that has been walked by our patriarchs, prophets and sages.

Before Adam was created, the Torah states, "All the bushes of the field had not yet grown, and the plants of the field had not yet sprung up, because God had not brought rain upon the earth, and there was no man to work the soil" (Genesis 2:5). This is speaking of the sixth day of creation, and Rashi notes that this seems to contradict the verse which says that on the third day, "the earth brought forth plants" (Genesis 1:12). Rashi explains that the plants only emerged as far as the surface of the ground, and there they remained until Adam prayed for rain. The rain then fell and all the plants and trees began to grow from the ground.

It is also taught that when Noah left the ark and saw the terrible destruction all around, he began to weep and cried out, "Lord of the Universe! You should have had mercy on Your creatures!"

---

1. Paraphrase of Psalms 34:13.
2. *Likutey Moharan* 9.
3. Paraphrase of Lamentations 2:19.

3

God replied to him, "Foolish shepherd! Now you are complaining! Earlier I told you, 'I have seen that you are righteous in this generation' (Genesis 7:1). I warned you, 'I am about to bring a killer flood upon the earth to destroy all life' (Genesis 6:17). I told you all that so you would pray for the world. Now that the world is destroyed, you are opening your mouth before Me with prayers and supplications!"

When Noah realized his mistake, he offered sacrifice and prayed to God for the future. The "appeasing fragrance" (Genesis 8:21) that God smelled was the fragrance of Noah's prayers.[4]

We also find many examples of Abraham's prayers. When God told Abraham, "The outcry of Sodom and Gomorrah is very great"(Genesis 18:20) and threatened to destroy the cities, Abraham immediatly "drew near"(Genesis 18:23) and began to pray and plead to God that He would spare the cities if fifty, or, finally even if ten righteous were to be found within their borders.

Our sages also comment on the verse, "Abraham got up early in the morning, and went to the place where he had stood before God" (Genesis 19:27). They say that this alludes to the fact that Abraham instituted a daily morning prayer.[5]

We also find that God said to Abimelech, "Return this man's wife, since he is a prophet and he will pray for you" (Genesis 20:7). The Torah then relates, "Abraham prayed to God, and God healed Abimelech" (Genesis 20:17). The Midrash notes that when Abraham offered this prayer, the knot was unbound.[6]

When Abraham's servant, Eliezer, went to find a bride for Isaac, he expressed his thoughts to God in prayer, and said, "God, Lord of my master Abraham, make me successful today, and do kindness to my master Abraham" (Genesis 24:12). The Midrash states that he said, "Lord of

---

4. *Zohar Chadash* 23a. Cf. *Zohar* 1:254b.
5. *Berakhoth* 26b.
6. *Bereshith Rabbah* 52:13.

the Universe! We are trying to complete what Abraham accomplished with his prayer when You granted him Isaac. Now complete that act of kindness and grant a wife for his son."[7]

Regarding Isaac, the Torah says, "Isaac went out to meditate in the field toward evening" (Genesis 24:63). The Talmud notes that this alludes to the fact that Isaac instituted a regular daily afternoon prayer.[8]

The Midrash states that Isaac was totally involved in prayer, and Rebecca said, "This is certainly a great man!" She therefore asked, "Who is this man walking in the field to meet us?" (Genesis 24:65).[9]

Later when Isaac married Rebecca and found her to be barren, the Torah states, "Isaac prayed for the sake of his wife" (Genesis 25:21). The Midrash[10] states that according to one opinion, he offered a wealth of prayer,[11] while others say that he prayed so much that he was able to overturn the decree with his prayer.[12]

The Torah says of Jacob, "He worshiped in that location" (Genesis 28:11). The Talmud states that from this we see that Jacob instituted a regular daily evening prayer.[13]

Jacob also prayed at length to God and said, "If God will be with me and watch me... giving me bread to eat and clothes to wear..." (Genesis 28:20). The Midrash states that God took the meditation of the Patriarchs and made it into the key for their descendants' redemption.[14]

The Midrash also notes that during the twenty years that Jacob was with Laban, he did not sleep nights, but recited the fifteen "songs of ascent" in the Psalms (120-134).[15] Jacob would spend entire nights meditating and praying to God.

---

7. *Bereshith Rabbah* 60:2.
8. *Berakhoth* 26b.
9. *Bereshith Rabbah* 60:15.
10. *Bereshith Rabbah* 63:5.
11. *Atar* (עטר) is seen as being the Aramaic for *Ashar* (עשר), denoting wealth.
12. *Atar* translated as a kind of pitchfork.
13. *Berakhoth* 26b.
14. *Bereshith Rabbah* 70:6.
15. *Bereshith Rabbah* 74:11.

When Jacob was returning to the Holy Land, he sent
emissaries to Esau. However, his main weapon was prayer,
and he said, "O God... Deliver me, I beg You, from the hand
of my brother, from the hand of Esau" (Genesis 32:12).

We also find that all the Matriarchs were constantly
involved in prayer. The Midrash says that God made the
Matriarchs barren because He desires the prayers of the
righteous.[16]

The Midrash also says that when Sarah was taken to
Abimelech's palace, she spent the entire night prostate on her
face, saying, "Lord of the Universe. . ."[17]

When Isaac was praying for Rebecca, the Torah says that
he prayed, "opposite his wife" (Genesis 25:21).[18] The
Midrash states that Isaac stood in one corner and prayed,
while Rebecca stood in the other corner and prayed.[19]

The Torah notes that Rachel said, "God has judged me
and has heard my prayer" (Genesis 30:6). She then said, "I
have been twisted around with my sister through all of God's
roundabout ways" (Genesis 30:8). Rashi explains that Rachel
did so with prayers that were precious to God.

When Rachel finally gave birth, the Torah says, "God
heard Rachel's [prayer] and He opened her womb" (Genesis
30:22). The Scripture later speaks of "Rachel weeping for her
children" (Jeremiah 31:15).

In describing Leah, the Torah says, "Leah's eyes were
tender" (Genesis 29:17). The Talmud teaches that they were
tender because she had wept and prayed so much that she
would not become Esau's wife.[20]

Jacob's sons were also involved in prayer. Thus, when
Jacob sent Benjamin with them to Egypt (Genesis 43:13), he
told his sons, "Here is the money, here are the tribute gifts,
and here is your brother."

16. *Bereshith Rabbah* 45:5. Cf. *Yevamoth* 64a.
17. *Bereshith Rabbah* 52:13.
18. Although this is usually translated, "for the sake of his wife," the word *nokhach* (נכח) more often has the connotation of "opposite" or "across from."
19. *Bereshith Rabbah* 63:5.
20. *Bava Bathra* 123a; *Bereshith Rabbah* 70:16.

"But it is your prayers that we need!" replied the sons.

"Then here is my prayer," said Jacob. "May God Almighty grant you mercy before the man (Genesis 43:14). May He who will eventually say 'enough' to all suffering now say 'enough' to my suffering."[21]

When Joseph was in prison in Egypt (Genesis 39:20), he also spent his time in prayer. We thus say the prayer, "May He who answered Joseph in prison also answer us!"[22]

When Joseph took Benjamin, the Torah says, "Judah approached" (Genesis 44:18). The Midrash comments that Judah approached God in prayer.[23]

When our ancestors were in Egypt, the Torah tells us that "The Israelites groaned because of their work, and they cried out, and their cry came up to God" (Exodus 2:23). At the Red Sea, it is similarly written, "Israel cried out to God" (Exodus 14:10).

Commenting on the verse, "My dove in the clefts of the rock, . . . let me hear your voice" (Song of Songs 2:14). The Midrash states that God is speaking to Israel, saying: "Let Me hear the same voice with which you cried out to Me in Egypt." From here we see that God desires the Israelites' prayers.[24]

Throughout the Torah and the works of our sages we find Moses constantly engaged in prayer and supplication, to God, both for himself and for Israel. When Israel sinned with the Golden Calf, "Moses entreated God" (Exodus 32:11). Moses later described his prayer, "I threw myself down in prayer before God for forty days and forty nights . . . (Deuteronomy 9:18).

The Midrash states that God taught Moses how to pray. At Marah God told Moses to say, "Make the bitter into the sweet." Later, when the Israelites sinned with the Golden Calf, Moses said to God, "Just as you told me at Marah to

---

21. *Bereshith Rabbah* 91:11, 92:1.
22. *Selichoth.*
23. *Bereshith Rabbah* 93:6.
24. *Shemoth Rabbah* 21:5.

pray that You make the bitter into the sweet, take the
bitterness of Israel's sin and make it sweet again."[25]

When Moses was praying for God to forgive the sin of
the Golden Calf, he kept praying until all his strength was
exhausted. He was willing to give up both this world and the
next for his people, as he said, "If [you do not forgive them]
obliterate me" (Exodus 32:32).[26]

When the Israelites sinned by listening to the spies,
Moses prayed for them (Numbers 14:13). When the people
grumbled against God, Moses prayed for them (Numbers
11:2). When Miriam was stricken with leprosy, Moses cried
out, "O God, please heal her!" (Numbers 12:13).

When it was decreed that Moses not enter the promised
land, Moses describes his response: "I supplicated (ve-eth-
chanan, ואתחנן) before God" (Deuteronomy 3:23). The
Midrash states that he offered 515 prayers, the numerical
value of ve-eth-chanan.[27] The Midrash concludes that if
Moses had offered one more prayer, he would have been
answered. The Midrash also speaks of the many prayers that
Moses said on the day that he died.[28]

Before sending Joshua as a spy, Moses prayed, "May
God protect you from the advice of the other spies."[29] When
Caleb saw that Moses did not pray for him, he made a point of
throwing himself on the grave of the Patriarchs to pray that
he would not be tempted to follow the other spies.[30]

After the rebellion of Korach, the Torah states that
"Aaron took the fire pan" (Numbers 17:12). At that time
Aaron offered many prayers to God to forgive the Israelites.
We thus say, "May He who answered Aaron with the fire
pan also answer us."[31]

25. *Shemoth Rabbah* 43:3.
26. *Zohar Chadash* 23a. Cf. *Berakhoth* 32a.
27. *Devarim Rabbah* 11:10.
28. *Ibid.*
29. *Sotah* 34b, from Numbers 13:16.
30. *Ibid.*, from Numbers 13:22.
31. *Selichoth.*

Similarly, when Pinchas stood up before the congregation (Numbers 25:7), he prayed, as it is written, "Pinchas stood up and prayed" (Psalms 106:30).

When the Israelites were defeated at Ai, "Joshua tore his clothes and fell to the earth on his face before the ark . . .and said, 'Alas, O Lord God . . .' " (Joshua 7:6,7).

In the days of the judges, whenever the Israelites sinned, God was angry with them and placed them in the hands of their enemies. Israel's response was to cry out to God,[32] until God had mercy on them, and raised up a judge to deliver them. This was true of each of the judges.

When the Philistines had put out Samson's eyes and bound him with brass fetters, Samson called out to God, "O God, Lord, remember me, I pray. Strengthen me this one more time!" (Judges 16:28).

When Hannah realized that God had sealed her womb, she wept and prayed to God at great length (1 Samuel 1:12). The Talmud states that from there we see that whoever prays at great length is answered.[33] It is also taught that whenever the righteous pray at length, they are answered.[34] Hannah said, "I have poured out my soul before God" (1 Samuel 1:15). She later said of Samuel, "This is the child for whom I prayed" (1 Samuel 1:27). The scripture records, "Hannah prayed and said . . ." (1 Samuel 2:1), upon which the Midrash comments, "She began to pray and confess."[35]

Later, when the Philistines had overpowered Israel, Samuel said, "Gather all Israel to Mitzpah and I will pray to God for you" (1 Samuel 7:5). The scripture says, "They went to Mitzpah and drew water, pouring it out before God" (1 Samuel 7:6). The commentaries note that they spilled out their hearts before God like water. It is then recorded, "Samuel cried out to God for Israel, and God answered him" (1 Samuel 7:9).

32. Judges 3:9, 3:15, 6:6, 10:10.
33. Shocher Tov. Cf. Yerushalmi, Taanith 4:1.
34. Yoma 29a.
35. Shocher Tov.

All the prophets also were constantly involved with praying. Elijah thus said, "God, Lord of Israel, before whom I stand, is life" (1 Kings 17:1). The commentaries note that he was saying that he was accustomed to standing before God in prayer.

When the son of the woman of Tzaraphath died, Elijah called out to God and said, "God my Lord, let this child's soul come back to him," and the scripture records that "God listened to Elijah's prayer" (1 Kings 17:21,22).

Similarly, at Mount Carmel, when he gathered all Israel along with the Baal's prophets to reveal that there is a God in Israel, Elijah approached God and said, "God, Lord of Abraham, Isaac and Israel, let it be known today that You are God in Israel . . . Answer me, God, answer me!" (1 Kings 19:36,37).

Although Elisha performed many miracles, the Talmud states, "Whatever Elisha accomplished, he did through prayer."[36]

When Jonah was swallowed by the giant fish, the scripture records that "Jonah prayed from the fish's belly" (Jonah 2:2). The scripture also records the "Prayer of Habakkuk" (Habakkuk 3:1).

It is written, "[God] hears the prayers of the righteous" (Proverbs 15:29). The Midrash comments that this is speaking of the prayers of the prophets of Israel.[37] It is written, "If they are prophets . . . let them pray to the Lord of Hosts" (Jeremiah 27:18).

King David spent his entire life engaged in prayers, supplication, and entreaty to God, expressing his thoughts to God until he was worthy of composing the Book of Psalms. It is thus taught that the verse, "[Noah] sent out the raven" (Genesis 8:7) refers to David who cried out to God like a raven. David would go out to the mountains like a raven to meditate, as it is written, "David climbed the ascent of the

---

36. *Megillah* 27a.
37. *Bereshith Rabbah* 52:5.

Mount of Olives, and he wept as he climbed, with his head covered" (2 Samuel 15:30).[38]

After King Solomon built the Holy Temple, he, too, prayed to God, as it is written, "Solomon stood before God's altar in the presence of the entire Israelite community, and he spread his hands (in prayer) to heaven" (1 Kings 8:22).

When King Hezekiah was sick, it is recorded that, "Hezekiah turned his face to the wall and prayed to God" (Isaiah 38:2). His prayer is then recorded at length.

When Daniel was asked to interpret King Nebuchadnezzar's dream, it is recorded, "Daniel went to his house and informed Chanania, Mishael and Azariah, his companions, so that they would pray to God in heaven concerning this secret" (Daniel 2:17,18).

Later, Darius made a law "that anyone who makes a petition to any god or man for the next thirty days . . . shall be cast into the lion's den" (Daniel 6:8). Daniel's response is recorded: "Daniel knew that the decree was signed, but he went to his house, and although the windows of his upstairs room were open to Jerusalem, he kneeled three times a day and prayed and gave thanks before his God, as he had always done" (Daniel 6:11).

When Daniel was then cast into the lions' den, he prayed with great intensity. We thus say, "May He who answered Daniel in the lions' den also answer us."[39]

Daniel also cried out to God regarding the destruction of Jerusalem, as he recorded, "I set my face to God, seeking Him with prayer, supplication, fasting, sackcloth and ashes. I prayed to God my Lord and confessed, saying, 'O Lord, the great and awesome God . . . Turn your ear, My God, and listen . . .' I thus spoke in prayer . . ." (Daniel 9:3 ff)

When Chanania, Mishael and Azariah were thrown into the fiery furnace, they were delivered only because they

---

38. *Zohar Chadash* 23c.
39. *Selichoth*.

prayed to God, as discussed in the Zohar.[40] We thus say, "May He who answered Chanania, Mishael and Azariah in the fiery furnace also answer us."[41]

Ezra similarly records, "I proclaimed a fast there at the Ahava River, so that we might humble ourselves before our God, and seek Him in a straight way . . . So we fasted and prayed to God . . . and He heard our prayer (Ezra 8:21, 23).

When he discovered that the Israelites had married gentile women, Ezra cried out bitterly and said, "I am ashamed and humiliated to lift my face to You, O God . . ." (Ezra 9:6). His entire prayer is then recorded.

When there was a decree against the Jews in Shushan, Mordecai and Esther prayed to God a great deal, as we see in the Book of Esther.[42]

Shortly after this, the Great Assembly ordained all the formal prayers that a person must address to God each day.

During the Talmudic period, all the sages would constantly engage in personal prayer. The Talmud thus records the prayers that many of the sages recited after the formal *Amidah*.[43] The sages also composed many prayers for special occasions, such as the traveler's prayer (*tefillath ha-derekh*).

They also ordained that before a person measures his grain, he should say, "May it be Your will, O God my Lord, that You send Your blessing in this pile of grain.[44] Similarly, before entering a city, one should say, "May it be Your will that You bring me into this city in peace."[45] After composing all these prayers, they finally said, "If only a person would pray all day long!"[46]

---

40. *Zohar* 3:57a.
41. *Selichoth*.
42. More is found in the Midrash and *Targum Sheni* (from text).
43. *Berakhoth* 17a.
44. *Bava Metzia* 42a.
45. *Berakhoth* 60a.
46. *Berakhoth* 21a.

In later times, many holy men composed prayers and poems (*piyutim*). Thus, the Ari[47] and his disciples composed a large number of prayers, such as those found in *Sha'arey Tzion*.[48]

The Baal Shem Tov also engaged constantly in meditation and revealed the importance of prayer, as we find in the works based on his teachings.

Rabbi Tzvi of Zidichov[49] writes:

> The best time to meditate is after midnight. One should rise and pray for his soul, which because of its sins, is so far from the Fountain of Life. At that time, he should review all that has passed, and speak out his heart, like a slave lying prostrate before his master.
>
> He should express his prayers like a child addressings its father. The language should be that which he usually speaks, so that his words will be fluent, and he will be able to express the pain in his heart for all the sins that he has committed, begging for forgiveness and atonement.
>
> The Zohar thus teaches, "Since the Holy Temple has been destroyed, the only thing left for us is prayer."[50] One should ask God to help him to worship, and to be in awe of the Divine with a perfect heart. One should pray in this manner at length; this is obviously more precious to God than any fast.

He then quotes a manuscript of *Beth Middoth*[51] attributed to the Ari, which states, "One must meditate,

---

47. "The Ari" was a popular name for Rabbi Yitzchak Luria (1534-1572), one of the most influential Kabbalists, and the leader of the Safed school of mysticism.

48. *Gates of Zion*, a collection of Kabbalistic and related prayers, by Rabbi Nathan Hanover (died 1683), a disciple of Rabbi Shlomo Edel's (the Maharsha). The book was first published in Prague, 1662, and republished in many subsequent editions.

49. Rabbi Tzvi Eichenstein of Zidichov (1763-1831) was a disciple of Rabbi Barukh of Medzeboz (grandson of the Baal Shem Tov), Rabbi Moshe Leib of Sasov, Rabbi Avraham Yehoshua Heshel of Apta, and the Koznitzer Maggid. The quotation is from *Sur MeRa VeAsseh Tov*, also known as *Hakdamah VeDerekh LeEtz Chaim*, first published in Lvov, 1832 (28 ff).

50. *Zohar* 3:124a.

51. This quotation from *Beth Middoth* appears originally in *Sefer Cheredim, Mitzvath HaTeshuvah* 3.

secluding himself with God. He must speak to God with quiet trepidation, as a slave speaks to his master, or a child to his father."

All the disciples of the Baal Shem Tov followed this path. Finally, the Baal Shem Tov's great-grandson, Rabbi Nachman of Breslov, renewed this ancient path which our ancestors had always followed, and he exceeded in prayer, supplication and meditation, in the fields and forests. It was he who enlightened us and taught us the proper way to follow this path. He told his followers, "Give me your hearts, and I will take you on a new path, which is really the old path upon which our fathers always walked."

HISHTAP'KKHUTH HA-NEFESH

1. Psalms and Repentance

If a person wishes to return to God, he must make it a habit to recite the Psalms (*Tehillim*). Reciting the Psalms is a specific practice that has the power to bring a person back to God.

There are 50 gates of return. Of these, 49 are gates through which every person can pass and gain access to what is beyond. the fiftieth gate, however, is that of God's own return, as it were. The concept of return is also seen as applying to God, as He said, "Return to Me, and I will return to you" (Malachi 3:7).

The 49 gates of return parallel the 49 letters in the Hebrew names of the 12 tribes of Israel.[1] Therefore, each gate of return is associated with one letter in the names of the tribes.

Every person has an inner desire to experience the awe of God. But not every person is worthy of returning to God. Even if a person has an inner awakening to return, he may not be able to reach the letter and gate that pertains to him. Moreover, even if he reaches the gate of return, he may find it closed. Thus, not everyone is worthy of returning.

However, if a person recites Psalms, even if he does not have any desire to return to God, such a desire can be awakened in him. Through the Psalms, he can become worthy of reaching the gate and letter that pertains to him, and even of opening the gate. Thus, through reciting Psalms, he can be worthy of truly returning to God.

This is alluded to in the verse (where King David calls himself) "the man who raised the yoke ... the sweet singer of Israel" (2 Samuel 23:1). The Talmud says that David called himself "the man who raised the yoke" because he was the one who had elevated the yoke of repentance and return to

---

1. The names of the twelve tribes of Israel are: ראובן שמעון לוי יהודה. יששכר זבולן יוסף בנימין
   דן נפתלי גד אשר They contain a total of 49 letters.

17

God.[2] However, he elevated the concept of repentance specifically because he was the "sweet singer of Israel," composing the Book of Psalms. This is because it is through the Psalms that a person can return to God.

The Talmud also teaches that King David was such a great saint that he never should have become involved with Bathsheba. God caused it to happen only to teach every individual how to repent.[3]

King David was therefore a paradigm of repentance. However, the main method that King David opened for repentance was the Book of Psalms. He composed them with such spirit and enlightenment that every person can find himself in the Psalms. By reciting the Psalms, he can then be worthy of returning to God.

As we have seen, the 49 gates of return parallel the 49 letters in the names of the Israel's sons, who gave rise to the twelve tribes of Israel. The main purification of the twelve tribes, where they gained access to the 49 gates of repentance, occurred in Egypt.

In Hebrew, Egypt is known as *Mitzraim* (מצרים). The name *Mitzraim* is associated with the word *metzar* (מצר), which means "narrowness of the throat,"[4] which is related to the concept of the higher type of repentance (*teshuvah ila'ah*).

It is for this reason that after the Israelites were purified in Egypt and were able to leave, they counted 49 days until they received the Torah at Sinai. These are the 49 days of the Omer, which parallel the 49 letters and the 49 gates of return, as discussed earlier.

Then on the 50th day of the Exodus, "God descended on Mount Sinai" (Exodus 19:20). This involved the concept regarding which God said, "I will return to you" (Malachi

---

2. *Moed Katan* 16b.
3. *Avodah Zarah* 4b.
4. *Shemonah Sha'arim, Shaar HaPesukim, VaYeshev.*

3:7). This is the return of God Himself, as it were, the fiftieth
gate of return.

All of this is alluded to in the verse, "These are the names
of Israel's sons who came to Egypt, each man with his
household" (Exodus 1:1). In the original Hebrew, "These are
the names of Israel's sons who came" is:

וְאֵלֶּה שְׁמוֹת בְּנֵי יִשְׂרָאֵל הַבָּאִים

The final letters of the words in this verse are התילם which can
be re-arranged to spell *tehillim* (תהילים), Hebrew for
Psalms.

The original Hebrew for the rest of the verse, "to Egypt,
each man with his household" is:

מִצְרָיְמָה אֵת יַעֲקֹב אִישׁ וּבֵיתוֹ

The final letters of the words here are התבשו which when re-
arranged spells *teshuvah* (תשובה), Hebrew for repentance
and return.

The lesson is that through Psalms one becomes worthy
of repentance. This is alluded to in the words, "These are the
names of Israel's sons." The 49 gates of return parallel the 49
letters in the names of Israel's sons, who came to Egypt to be
purified there.

We therefore see that in times of repentance, such as
during Elul[5] and the Ten Days of Repentance,[6] it is a custom
among Jews to recite the Psalms. As we said earlier, reciting
Psalms is a specific practice that can bring one to repentance.
It is therefore a very great thing to recite Psalms constantly.
The Psalms can be a source of tremendous awakening toward
God. Happy is the one who grasps this method.

Likutey Moharan Tinyana 73

Many people have no idea how to reach the specific gate
of repentance through which they can return to God.

---

5. Elul is the month preceding Rosh HaShanah.
6. The days between Rosh HaShanah and Yom Kippur.

However, through reciting Psalms, one can reach the gate of repentance that pertains to his soul.

Likutey Etzoth, s.v. Teshuvah 32

From the Rebbe's words, it appears that the 49 gates he discusses are 49 ways of returning to God. According to the root of each person's soul, he has a specific path and a specific service through which he can return to God. This is discussed by the Rebbe, in his explanation of the teaching, "[Man in this world] is like a person traveling in the pitch dark night . . . who does not know which path to take."[7] There he explains that not every person is worthy of finding the particular path that relates to the root of his soul.

Regarding this, King David cried out, "How shall a young person purify his path? Only by taking heed according to Your word" (Psalms 119:9). The Rebbe revealed that through reciting the Psalms (*Tehillim*), God will grant him wisdom, understanding and knowledge so as to enable him to find the specific path that pertains to him according to the root of his soul. He will then know what he must do in order to return to God completely.[8]

2. Meditation

Meditation is the highest path of all. One must therefore set aside an hour or more each day to meditate by himself in a room or in the field.

Meditation should consist of conversation with God. One can pour out his words before his Creator. This can include complaints, excuses, or words seeking grace, acceptance and reconciliation. He must beg and plead that God bring him close and allow him to serve Him in truth.

One's conversation with God should be in the everyday language that he normally uses. Hebrew may be the preferred language for prayer, but it is difficult for a person to express

---

7. *Sotah* 21a. This is discussed in *Likutey Moharan* 4:8.
8. See *Likutey Halakhoth, Keriath Sh'ma* 5.

himself in Hebrew. Furthermore, if one is not accustomed to speaking Hebrew, his heart is not drawn after the words.

However, in the language that a person normally speaks, it is very easy for him to express himself. The heart is closer to such a language, and follows it, since the person is more accustomed to it. Therefore, when one uses his native language, he can express everything that is in his heart, and tell it to God.

One's conversation with God can consist of regret and repentance. It can consist of prayers and pleading to be worthy of approaching Him and coming close to Him in truth from this day on. Each one should speak to God according to his own level.

One must be very careful to accustom himself to spend at least one hour a day in such meditation. During the rest of the day, one will then be in a state of joy and ecstasy.

This practice is extremely potent and powerful. It is an extremely beneficial practice in coming close to God. It is a general practice that is all-inclusive.

No matter what one feels he is lacking in his relationship to God, he can converse with God and ask him for help. This is true even if one is completely removed from any relationship with God.

There will be many times that one will find it impossible to say anything to God. His mouth will be sealed, and he will not be able to find any words to say. Nevertheless, the very fact that he has made the effort and has prepared himself to converse with God is in itself very beneficial. He has tried, and is ready and prepared to converse with God, yearning and longing to do so, but he is unable. This in itself is also very good.

Actually, one can make a conversation and prayer out of this itself. He should cry out to God that he is so far from Him that he cannot even speak. He should beg that God grant him mercy and open his mouth, so that he will be able to express himself before Him.

Many great holy men have related that they reached their high spiritual level only through this practice. An intelligent person will realize that with this practice one can constantly reach higher and higher. Furthermore, it is a universal practice that can be used by great and small alike. Every individual can make use of this practice, and reach the highest levels. Happy is he who grasps it.

It is also good to make prayers out of lessons. Thus if one hears a Torah lesson from a true holy man, he should make it into a prayer. He should contemplate everything in the lesson, and pray to God that he be worthy of attaining it. He should tell God how far he is from such attainment, and beg that he be helped to achieve everything in the lesson.

If one then has intelligence and true desire, God will guide him along the path of truth, and he will understand how to reach his goal. He will speak with beautiful words and true arguments, pleading with God to draw him close to Him.

The concept of conversation with God is bound to an extremely high spiritual level. This is especially true when one makes prayers out of Torah lessons. This results in great delight on high.

Likutey Moharan Tinyana 25

If one wishes to make a Torah lesson into a prayer, he should particularly try to do so with the lessons found in the Rebbe's works. These are lessons in which each person can find himself.

Time passes quickly, and we have no way to the eternal except through prayers and supplications. The main practice is this ancient new way, which involves making Torah lessons into prayers.

A person may feel that he is very far from this path. But this is not-so. "It is something that is very close to you—in your mouth and your heart, so that you can do it" (Deuteronomy 30:14).

Even if one cannot begin to speak at all, we have a number of methods which are tried and tested, and have already helped us very much.

Alim LeTerufah 257

3. Meditation and Weeping

We have spoken of meditation and expressing oneself before God, as well as reciting Psalms, supplications, and prayers. It is very good if one is worthy of saying them with a true perfect heart until he is weeping before God, just as a child weeps before its parent.

However, if a person recites Psalms, supplications or prayers, and tries to make himself weep, it is not good. Rather, it confuses the mind so that he cannot recite the prayers in a true meditative state.

When a person is saying any supplication or prayer, he must divest himself of all external thoughts, focusing his mind exclusively on the words that he is speaking before God. He should thus be like a person speaking to his friend.[9]

If he does this, his heart will be aroused until he automatically begins to weep with true tears. However, if one tries to cause himself to weep, he will not be successful in the correct manner. His very meditation will be confused by this, as mentioned earlier.

If one even thinks that he will weep, this too is an extraneous thought, which destroys his mental focus. He then cannot hear what he is saying. The main thing is to speak before God in truth, without any other thoughts in mind at all. If one is then worthy of weeping, it is fine, and if not, not. But he should not confuse his meditation with this.

Likutey Moharan Tinyana 95

---

9. Paraphrasing Exodus 33:11.

4. Repeating One Word

It is very important to meditate and to express one's thoughts before God each day.

If one cannot speak at all, then he should say a single word, and this is also very good.

If one can only say one word, he should remain mentally strong, and repeat that word over and over again, countless times. He can spend many days meditating with that word, and that in itself is very good.

If he is persistent and repeats that word countless times, God will have mercy and open his mouth, so that he will be able to express his thoughts.

Speech has a very great power. If one knows how, he can say a word to a gun so that it will not shoot. Understand this.

It would be great if a person could spend the entire day meditating. However, not every person can do this. Therefore, it is mandatory that a person spend at least a few hours each day in meditation.

If one's mind is strong, and he wants to accept upon himself the true yoke of God, he must spend the entire day in meditation. This is alluded to in the Talmudic saying, "If a person would only pray all day long!"[10]

Likutey Moharan Tinyana 96

5. Blazing a New Trail

There is another advantage in expressing one's own thoughts before God in one's meditation. One can meditate by reciting supplications and prayers that have already been composed. However, all the forces that destroy one's meditative state and denounce it lie along the path of such prayers. This is because these forces are well aware of such paths.

---

10. *Berakhoth* 21a.

It is very much like a well known public road. Since bandits and murderers are aware of this road, they can lurk alongside it, waiting for the unwary. But if one blazes a new trail, or travels one that is not yet known, then no unfriendly elements can lurk on the wayside.

Similarly, when a person expresses his own thoughts to God, he is taking a new path and composing a new prayer. Therefore, he is not nearly as likely to encounter negative forces.

Nevertheless, one must also make other prayers and supplications part of one's meditations.

Likutey Moharan Tinyana 97

6. Opening the Heart

Speech has a great power to awaken a person spiritually.

Sometimes a person thinks that he has no heart and cannot reach a meditave state. Nevertheless, if he expresses himself with many words of awakening, supplication and prayer, this speech itself will bring a revelation and awakening of his meditative powers and his soul.

This is the meaning of the verse, "My soul came forth when he spoke" (Song of Songs 5:6). It indicates that speech itself is a revelation of the soul and the heart.

It often happens that if one speaks to God very much, even without any true meditation, he can arrive at a great revelation of his meditative powers and his soul. This is because speech itself has great power.

Likutey Moharan Tinyana 98

7. Limits of Meditation

True meditation and self-expression before God comes when one has done so to such a degree that he feels that his soul is about to leave him and he is about to die. His soul is then bound to the body by nothing more than a hairlike thread, due to the great longing and desire that he has toward God.

The Talmud speaks of this and says, "A person's prayer is not heard on high unless he places his soul in his hands."[11]

When a person meditates, he is helped by God. He can then express his thoughts before God just as a person speaks to a friend. One must accustom himself to converse with God just as he would with his teacher or friend. "The whole world is filled with His glory" (Isaiah 6:3), and God can be found in every place.

Likutey Moharan Tinyana 99

8. Self Perfection

No man, whether great or small, can perfect himself except through meditation.

The Rebbe spoke of many true holy men, and said that all of them reached their high spiritual levels only through meditation.

Once he spoke of a simple man who was a grandson of the Baal Shem Tov. He said that this man was also constantly expressing his thoughts before God with profuse weeping. He explained that this is particularly true of the Baal Shem Tov's descendants, since the Baal Shem Tov himself was a direct descendant of King David. David's entire mode of service was to make his heart contrite before God at all times. This is the foundation of the Book of Psalms that he composed.

Likutey Moharan Tinyana 100

9. The Midnight Prayer

In the Midnight Prayer (*Tikkun Chatzoth*, תקון חצות), one can express everything in his heart just as he does in meditation. Although the Midnight Prayer speaks of the destruction of the Holy Temple, it is not speaking only of the past. The main reason for saying the Midnight Prayer is because of what is currently happening. Therefore, when a

---

11. *Taanith* 8a.

person says the Midnight Prayer, he can find everything in his heart in the words.

The same is true when one recites the Psalms. Here too, one must see himself in each Psalm. This is also true of other standard prayers and supplications that he may say. Very easily, without any forced interpretation, one can find himself in the simple meaning of all prayers and supplications.

This is especially true of the Psalms, which were said for all Israel, and include each individual. No matter what battles a person may have with his personal urges, they are all expressed in the Psalms.

Although the Psalms appear to be speaking of mundane wars, the entire book is speaking primarily about the war with the Evil Urge (*Yetzer HaRa*, יצר הרע) and its armies. These are a person's true enemies, and they can keep him from the path of life and bring him down to the deepest pit, if he is not careful to avoid them.

It is regarding this that the book of Psalms was written. Therefore, the primary way to come close to God is only through reciting the Psalms and other prayers, and by meditating and expressing one's thoughts before God. One must beg that God draw him close. The only way that one can win this war is if he is strong and brave, constantly praying to God, no matter what happens. He will then certainly win the great battle. Happy is he.

From the words of the Rebbe, we understood that, although many paths to God are discussed in his works, most of them are very difficult to follow. Therefore, the main path of each person is that of prayer. Whatever the situation, one must speak out, no matter how, and ask God to bring him from darkness to light and to help him attain true repentance.

One must not stop until he is answered. Even if one calls to God for a long time, and still finds himself very, very far from him, he should remain strong and firm in his prayers. If he does so, he can be certain that God will ultimately answer him, and draw him close so that he will be able to serve God in truth. This is an absolute certainty, without any doubt whatsoever.

Our sages thus teach, "Prayer requires strengthening, as it is written, 'Pray to God! Be strong and brave, and pray to God' (Psalms 27:14)."[12] Rashi explains that this means that if one's prayer is not accepted, he must pray again. One must continue doing so until God looks down and sees. It is thus written, "Israel, hope in God now and forever" (Psalms 131:3).

Although we have discussed this many times, we must repeat it again and again each day. The many things that can weaken and confuse a person are beyond description. Therefore, we must repeat a thousand times how we must stay firm and pray to God constantly, begging Him to bring us closer to Him, no matter what.

"Let us lift our hearts with our hands to God in heaven" (Lamentations 3:41). "God will not forsake His people nor forsake His heritage" (Psalms 94:14). "God's mercies have not come to an end, for his compassion is never-ending" (Lamentations 3:22).

Likutey Moharan Tinyana 101

10. Isolation

When a person is meditating and praying, it is not good if he hears other people. He must not hear any other person, or even be aware that another person is standing in the vicinity.

During prayer and meditation a person must imagine that nothing else exists other than himself and God.

Elsewhere[13] the Rebbe said that a person must nullify himself so much during prayer that he is not aware of himself at all. His entire awareness is then of God.

Likutey Moharan Tinyana 103

---

12. *Berakhoth* 32b.
13. *Likutey Moharan* 55.

11. Simplicity

The Rebbe was very fond of the simple worship of ordinary religous people. He liked very much when a person was able to recite the many optional prayers found in the larger prayer books, recited by many simple people.

On many occasions, he told us to be careful to sing the Sabbath table hymns (*zemiroth* , זמירות). He would become very upset and angry with those who thought themselves too sophisticated to make the effort to sing these table hymns at the Sabbath meals and at the close of the Sabbath.

The same was true of other simple worship. The essence of Judaism is simplicity and absolute innocence, without any sophistication.

Before the Rebbe contracted the sickness[14] that would take his life, he would sing the table hymns at the Sabbath meals and at the close of the Sabbath.

Likutey Moharan Tinyana104

12. Learning

Once a person asked the Rebbe what practices he should use to draw close to God. The Rebbe told him to learn certain Torah subjects. When the person said that he did not have the ability to learn these subjects, the Rebbe responded that through prayer one can accomplish everything. With prayer one can gain all good, whether learning, the ability to worship, holiness, or any other good that might exist in all the spiritual universes.

Once the Rebbe said, "If a person could come back from the dead and pray, he would certainly pray with all his might."

Likutey Moharan Tinyana 111

---

14. Tuberculosis, which he contacted on his journey to Navarich, some four years before his death.

13. Attachment

The main concept of prayer is attachment (*devekuth*, דבקות) to God.

Because of this, in many ways it would be better even to worship in the vernacular. When one prays in the language that he commonly speaks, his heart is very close to the words of the prayer service, and can be attached to the words. Through this, one would be able to attach himself even more closely to God.

However, the men of the Great Assembly[15] canonized an order of prayer service in Hebrew, and we must recite it in that language.

Still, the main thing is to concentrate on the simple meaning of the words. This is the main concept of worship, where we pray to God for all things. Through this, one can attain a mystical attachment to God.

(There are some people who make use of Kabbalistic meditations involving the words of worship service. If one is not ready for this, he can cause himself great spiritual damage.)[16]

If a person speaks Hebrew as his native language, he need not make a special effort to have the meaning of the words in mind. Rather, he should merely pay attention to the words that he is saying. This is the main focus (*kavanah*, כוונה) that one must have during prayer.

In the case of the truly great saints (*tzaddikim*, צדיקים), all the Kabbalistic meditations found in the writings of the Ari[17] were included in the simple meaning of the words. For them, the simple meaning of the words could include all Kabbalistic meditations.

Likutey Moharan Tinyana 120

---

15. The Great Assembly (*Kenesseth HaGedolah*) was the supreme council and court (*Sanhedrin*) in the time of Ezra, right after the building of the Second Temple.
16. Discussed in detail in *Likutey Moharan* 120.
17. A popular name for Rabbi Yitzchak Luria (1534-1572), one of the most influencial Kabbalists, and head of the Safed school.

14. Encouragement

The Rebbe would constantly give encouragement to those who came to him and complained that they were far from true prayer, and that they found it very difficult to pray. He would encourage them and comfort them in every way possible so that they would not become discouraged.

He would often say, "A person can find comfort and joy in the fact that he is worthy of saying the words of the worship service."

I once heard the Rebbe speaking with a simple man, who found it difficult to pray with feeling. The Rebbe told him that he should only recite the preliminary prayers, before *Barukh She-amar,*[18] with feeling. It is possible that in this incarnation (*gilgul,* גלגול),[19] he needed only to rectify that part of the service, since the rest of the service had already been rectified in previous incarnations. In this incarnation, he only had to recite the parts before *Barukh She-amar* with concentration and feeling. He should therefore place his entire effort to concentrate on the portion of the service before *Barukh She-amar.*

Once this has been accomplished, such a person should consider that the portion of the service that he must rectify is that from *Barukh She-amar* to *Va Ye-bharekh David.*[20] He should then recite that portion with great concentration and feeling.

One can continue in this manner throughout the entire worship service.

In general then, one should not confuse himself by trying to perfect the entire service at once. Rather, he should make an effort to say at least a little with proper concentration. Obviously, it is always possible to concentrate

18. *Barukh She-Amar* ("Blessed is He who Spoke") is the prayer that introduces the "Psalms of Praise" (*Pesukey DeZimra*) in the daily Morning Service.
19. Parts of souls are reincarnated so as to rectify misdeeds from previous lives.
20. *VaYe-bharekh David* ("And David Blessed") consists of a reading from 1 Chronicles 29:10-13, and it concludes the "Psalms of Praise" in the morning service.

on a small section of the service. Then, little by little, one can add other portions.

Likutey Moharan Tinyana 121

Elsewhere in the Rebbe's writings, [21] it is explained that in most cases, one cannot recite the entire service properly, but only a small part of it. This is because each person can only properly recite the part of the service that relates to his spiritual state. Thus, "there are masters of hands, and masters of feet." [22]

Since each person can concentrate on the portion of the service that relates to his spiritual state, one should not be discouraged if he finds himself concentrating properly on only a small portion of the service. Sometimes he may have good concentration, and suddenly, it breaks off, and he cannot worship properly, no matter how he tries. Sometimes, this is the way things must be, as discussed earlier.

Therefore, in such a case, one should make every effort to recite the rest of the service with absolute simplicity. Through this, God will help him to arouse himself so that he will be able to recite the rest of the service with proper alertness.

Even if one is not worthy of spiritual arousal during the entire service, what is done is done. If he is worthy, he may still try to recite a Psalm or other optional prayer with intense concentration.

Every person is aware of his shortcomings. He must therefore realize that he is very far from the concept of prayer, which is very, very high. How can he be worthy of such a high level of service?

Therefore, each person must merely do his part. He should recite the words of the service with absolute simplicity, paying careful attention to what he is saying. In

---

21. *Sichoth HaRan* 75, translated as *Rabbi Nachman's Wisdom.*
22. *Tikuney Zohar* 18. Various parts of the service parallel various parts of the body.

most cases, he will then automatically begin to have proper concentration and alertness.

Elsewhere,[23] the Rebbe states that a person must strengthen himself in prayer even when he is not worthy of praying with spiritual attachment, and when his prayer is not fluent. At such times in particular, he should strengthen himself to pray with all his might and with full concentration. When one is then worthy of praying with spiritual attachment and fluency, he can elevate all his other prayers with the one recited properly.

This is alluded to in Moses' words, "I pleaded with God at that time, saying..." (Deuteronomy 3:23). Moses was saying, "I pleaded with God at all times, whether with spiritual attachment or without. But 'at that time saying.' When I was worthy of praying with attachment and fluency, I was able to elevate even the prayers that I said improperly along with those said with proper concentration.

In another place,[24] the Rebbe says that a person's prayers are sometimes devoid of enthusiasm and feeling. At such times, one must arouse his won emotions and make the words burn like a fire in his heart.

A person can sometimes work himself up and make himself angry. People say, "He is working himself up into a rage." One must do the same during prayer, and be like the person who makes himself angry. One can work himself up and bring emotion and feeling into his prayer.

The enthusiasm may be forced at first, but it will eventually become real. The heart will seem to burst aflame with God's praise, and the person will be worthy of experiencing true prayer.

---

23. *Likutey Moharan* 99.
24. *Sichoth HaRan* 74.

15. Place

Sometimes a person has thoughts of repentance and a desire for God in a certain place. Right there in that place, the person must then strengthen himself with thoughts of repentance and a desire for God. That is, he must say a few words of prayer, or verbally express his spiritual desire and longing, depending on the context. He should not wait or leave that spot.

This is true even if the particular place is not especially conducive to prayer. One may have such thoughts and feelings when he is not in a synagogue or house of Torah study, but on the road or the like. Nevertheless, once he moves, he can interrupt the thought and lose it.

We saw the Rebbe himself follow the above advice many times.

Likutey Moharan Tinyana 124

16. Finding Oneself in the Psalms

When one recites Psalms, the main thing is to say each Psalm for himself.

Although the Psalms appear to be speaking of wars, the wars in the Psalms are those that each individual must fight against the Evil Urge and his troops.[25]

A man once asked the Rebbe how can a person identify himself with the Psalms where King David praises himself, such as the verse, "Keep my soul because I am a saint" (Psalms 86:2)?

The Rebbe replied that one must identify even with such Psalms. One must give himself the benefit of the doubt and seek in himself whatever merit and good points he can find. In these points every person can be a saint.

The Rebbe then explained that the scripture says of Jehoshafat, "His heart was lifted up in the ways of God" (2

---

25. See #9.

Chronicles 17:6). If one wants to walk God's paths and truly serve him, he must lift his heart to some degree.

The Rebbe also said that at the beginning of the worship service, we say, "What are we? What are our lives? ..."[26] where we denigrate ourselves. However, we then say, "But we are the children of Your covenant..." We then strengthen ourselves even more, and speak of our greatness that we are God's people, the descendants of Abraham, Isaac and Jacob.

This is what one must always do when serving God.[27]

Likutey Moharan Tinyana 125

17. Pouring Out One's Thoughts

It is very good to pour out one's thoughts[28] before God, like a child pleading before its parent.[29]

God calls us His children, as it is written, "You are children to God your Lord" (Deuteronomy 14:1). Therefore, it is good to express one's thoughts and troubles to God, as a child complains to his father and pesters him.

One may think that he has done so much wrong that he is no longer one of God's children. Still, he must remember that God always calls him His child. We are taught, "Whether good or evil, you are always called His children."[30]

Even if God has dismissed you and told you that you are no longer His child, you must still say, "Let Him do as He wills. But I must do my part and still behave like His child."

It is very good if one can awaken his heart and plead until tears stream from his eyes, so that he stands like a child weeping before his Father.

Sichoth HaRan 7

---

26. In *LeOlam Yehey Adam*, a prayer said after the morning blessings.
27. Also see *Likutey Moharan Tinyana 282*, translated in *Rabbi Nachman's Fire*.
28. Cf. *Psalms* 142:3.
29. Cf. *Taanith* 3:8 (19a).
30. *Kiddushin* 36a.

In a letter,[31] Rabbi Nathan[32] discusses the verse, "Is
Ephraim a darling son to Me? Is he a dandled child? As often
as I speak of him, I recall him and My heart yearns for him..."
(Jeremiah 31:20). The Midrash[33] cites a debate as to whether
a "dandled child" denotes one who is two or three years old,
or if it is speaking of a four or five year old.

The commentaries note that according to those who
maintain that the verse is speaking of a two or three year old,
the child in question is so young that it cannot speak except
with a few stunted words or half-expressions. Nevertheless,
the parent delights in the child's words and tries to satisfy the
child's desires.

According to the opinion that the child is four or five,
the verse is speaking of a child who can actually ask his parent
to give him something, so that the parent can fulfill its
request.

Although the concept is not very clear, I explained the
words somewhat more deeply and gained great
encouragement. The Rebbe told us that we must converse
with God each day, and this Midrash gave me much strength.

From the teaching, we can see that even if a person
cannot speak at all before God, and finds it impossible to
express his thoughts, he is still precious in God's eyes. This is
true even if a person can only speak in hints and half-phrases
like a two or three year old child. Sometimes God helps the
person, and he can then express his thoughts more clearly,
like a four or five year old.

Therefore, it is very precious before God when people try
to speak to Him. The verse, "As often as I speak of him," can
also be translated, "it is enough that My speech is in him."[34]
From here we see that the power of speech is so great that it

31. *Alim LeTerufah* 254.
32. Rabbi Nathan of Nemerov (1780-1840) was the foremost disciple of Rabbi
Nachman, and the editor of most of his works.
33. *VaYikra Rabbah* 2.
34. In Hebrew, the verse says מדי דבר בו which can be interpreted as די דבורי בו.

cannot be put into writing; therefore we must allude to it in just a few words.

However, from all this, one can understand enough to strengthen himself in his speech and meditation before God. Of course, it is best to speak clearly before God. But if one cannot speak clearly, even the broken phrases of a two or three year old are very precious in God's eyes.

One must keep this in its simple sense, since it is our eternal life. It is impossible to pass through this world without it, since our only power is that of speech.

18. Happiness and Contrition

When a person is happy all day long, it is easy to set aside some time each day when he can express his thoughts before God with a contrite heart. But when one is depressed, it is very difficult to meditate and to speak to God.

Sichoth HaRan 20

19. True Contrition

Contrition is in no way related to sadness and depression. Depression comes from the side of evil, and is hateful to God. A contrite heart, on the other hand, is very dear and precious to God.

It would be very good to be contrite and broken-hearted all day long. For the average person, however, this could easily degenerate into depression.

One must therefore set aside some time each day for contrition. At a given time each day, he should meditate before God with a contrite heart. The rest of the day should then be joyful.

Sichoth HaRan 41

20. Depression and Contrition

Depression is like anger and rage, like a complaint against God because He is not fulfilling one's wishes.

Contrition, on the other hand, is the feeling that a child has when it pleads to its parent. One is then like a baby, weeping and complaining because his parent is far away.

Sichoth HaRan 42

21. The Joy of Contrition

After true contrition comes joy. A sign of true contrition is when one is later truly happy.

Sichoth HaRan 45

22. Daily Meditation

One must be very worthy in order to be able to meditate for a given time each day and regret what he must.

Not everyone can be worthy of doing this. The days pass and are gone, and one finds that his life is over and he never once had time to think about the meaning of his life.

One must therefore make sure to set aside a specific time each day to review his life calmly. He should consider what he is doing, and ponder whether it is something worthy of one's devotion.

Sichoth HaRan 47

23. Meditation in Bed

King David was able to compose the Book of Psalms only because he was very strong in meditation.

The main time that King David would meditate was at night, under his bedcovers. Hidden from the sight of all others, he would pour out his heart before God. He thus said, "Every night I meditate in tears upon my bed" (Psalms 6:7).

Happy is one who can follow this practice, since it is the highest of all.

Sichoth HaRan 67

The Rebbe also discussed the idea that when a person lies down to sleep each night, he should express his thoughts to God and pray that he should be worthy of coming close to

Him and serving Him. If he cannot speak to God because his heart is too hard, he should still moan and sigh because he is so far from God. He will then be worthy of coming closer to Him.

24. Conquering God

The Talmud says, "Sing to the One who rejoices when conquered."[35] This indicates that there are times when one must even conquer God.

One may feel that he is rejected by God because of his sins. But even if one feels that he is not doing God's will, he should still remain strong and depend on God's mercy. One should spread his hands before God and beg that He have mercy and let him serve Him in truth.

A person may feel rejected by God, but he still must cry out, "It doesn't matter! I want to be a Jew!"

This is how one can overcome God. God has great joy when He is overcome in this manner.

Sichoth HaRan 69

As a result of the joy that God has from this, He sends a person words so that the person can conquer Him. Without this, it would obviously be impossible for mere flesh and blood to conquer God. It is only possible because God Himself helps the person.

Likutey Moharan 124

25. God's Attention

When a person wishes to speak to God and express his thoughts before Him, asking that he be brought close so as to serve Him, then, as it were, God puts aside all His concerns. He throws aside any evil decree that He may wish to bring about, and all His other affairs, as it were. He turns Himself exclusively to the person who wishes to express his thoughts

---

35. *Pesachim* 119a.

and ask that God help him come closer and serve Him. As a result, Israel is then saved from all evil decrees.

Sichoth HaRan 70

26. Good News

When one hears good news, it helps him to be able to recite Psalms.

Sichoth HaRan 97

27. Psalms and the Divine Breath

When one recites Psalms, it is as great as if King David himself were reciting them.

King David wrote the Psalms with divine inspiration. In Hebrew this is known as *ruach ha-kodesh* (רוח הקדש), which can also be translated as "Divine Breath."

This Divine Breath is still in the words of the Psalms. Therefore when a person recites the Psalms, his own breath awakens the Divine in the words. When one recites the Psalms, it is therefore as if King David himself were chanting them.

If a person is ill, it is very beneficial for him to trust only in God. He should have faith that reciting the Psalms will help him.

Faith is a support and a staff. One can lean and depend on God just at one leans on a staff or cane. King David therefore said, "God has been my Staff" (Psalms 18:19). David could lean on God, just as on a physical support.

The Torah says of an injured person, "If he rises and walks about with his *staff*, he shall be cleared" (Exodus 21:19). This indicates that one is healed through the staff of faith.

It is written, "A *staff* shall come forth out of the stock of Jesse" (Isaiah 11:1). This verse is speaking of the Messiah, who will be a descendant of King David. He will be the one to hold the staff of faith.

It is also written, "The *breath* of our nostrils, God's Messiah" (Lamentations 4:20). The staff of healing used by the Messiah will arise through the Divine Breath that King David placed in the Psalms.

Regarding the Messianic age, it is written, "For many days, old men and women will sit in the broad places of Jerusalem, each with his *staff* in his hand" (Zechariah 8:4). From this verse, the Talmud derives the teaching that the righteous will resurrect the dead in the Messianic age.[36] The staff that the righteous will hold will be that which Elisha used to resurrect the son of the Shunnamite woman, regarding which he said, "You shall place the staff on the boy's face" (2 Kings 4:31). This is the healing staff of faith.

Winter is pregnancy and summer is birth. In the winter all plants and grasses seem to die. Their strength is dissipated, and they are like the dead. But when the summer comes, they awaken and return to life.

It is written, "Isaac went out to meditate (*su'ach*, שוח) in the field" (Genesis 24:63). The Talmud teaches that this meditation was prayer.[37]

When summer begins, it is very good to meditate in the fields. It is a time when one can pray to God with yearning and longing.

Meditation and prayer is *sichah* (שיחה). A bush of the field is a *si'ach* (שיח). Thus, when every bush of the field begins to return to life and grow, they all yearn to be included in prayer and meditation.

Sichoth HaRan 98

It is for this reason that Isaac meditated especially in the field. His prayer was with every bush of the filed, wehre every bush brought its power into his prayer.

Likutey Moharan Tinya 1

---

36. *Pesachim* 68a; *Zohar* 1:114b, 135a.
37. *Berakhoth* 26b.

28. The Song of the Field

How wonderful it would be if one could only be worthy of hearing the song of the grass. Each blade of grass sings out to God without any ulterior motive and without expecting any reward. It is most wonderful to hear its song and worship God in its midst.

The best place to meditate is in a field where things grow. There one can truly express his thoughts before God.

Sichoth Haran 163

The best place to meditate is in the meadows outside the city. One should meditate in a grassy field, for grass will awaken the heart.

Sichoth Haran 227

29. Hanging by a Thread

Imagine that you are in the middle of the sea, with a storm raging to the very heart of the heavens. You are hanging by a thin thread, and do not know how to save yourself. You cannot even cry out to God. The only thing you can do is lift your eyes and heart to God.

You should place yourself in such a state of mind whenever you meditate and cry out to God. Deep in your soul, you are aware of the great danger that exists everywhere in this world.

Sichoth HaRan 117

30. From the Maw of the Depths

I was once standing before the Rebbe as he lay sick in bed. He said, "The main lesson is, 'from the maw of the depths I cried out' (Jonah 2:3)."

Sichoth HaRan 302

A person can fall so low in his own esteem that he thinks that our advice does not pertain to him at all. He is then like a person who has descended into the "maw of the depths." He feels that he has cried out to God very much, and it has not helped him. Such negative thoughts can totally overwhelm a person.

But this is never true. The Rebbe's lessons apply to all people, no matter how low they think they have fallen.

Alim LeTerufah 60

31. Special Practices

There are specific practices that each individual must keep in order to rectify the spiritual damage that he has done, each one according to the root of his soul.

However, the practice of meditating and expressing one's thoughts to God each day in one's own native tongue is a universal practice. Every Jew must do this every day of his life.

Another universal practice is the daily study of the *Shulchan Arukh,*[38] the primary code of Jewish law.

Sichoth HaRan 185

32. Confusion

There are certainly many virtuous people who do not meditate, but inwardly they are confused and confounded. If the Messiah were to summon them suddenly, without warning, they would be mixed up and confused.

When a man wakes up from a restful sleep, his mind is calm and relaxed. This is how a person who meditates will be when the Messiah arrives. He will not be confused or confounded.

Sichoth HaRan 228

---

38. The *Shulchan Arukh* ("Prepared Table") written by Rabbi Yosef Caro (1488-1575) is the accepted code of Jewish law.

33. Yearning

Your heart should be drawn to God so strongly that even when you are among people, you feel great emotion toward God. You wish to lift your hands and heart to God, and with deep yearning and intense emotions, cry out to Him, "Do not forsake me, O God my Lord" (Psalms 38:22).

When the Rebbe related this, he lifted his hands with great emotion and deep yearning, and recited this verse.

Sichoth HaRan 230

34. Depression and Heartbreak

There is a vast difference between depression and a broken heart. When one has a broken heart, he can be standing in the middle of a crowd, and turn around and say, "Master of the world..."

When the Rebbe spoke of this, he then raised his hands with great emotion, and said, "Master of the world!"

Sichoth HaRan 231

35. The Spider Web

You are like a warrior who is prepared to breach a mighty wall. But when you come to the gate, you find it blocked by a spider web. If you returned in defeat because of the spider web blocking your path, you would be the most foolish of men.

The parallel is obvious. The main thing is speech. Use it and you will win every spiritual battle.

You can meditate in thought, but the most important thing is to express your thoughts in speech.

The parable teaches a most important lesson. You might find it difficult to speak to God. But this difficulty is mere foolishness. It indicates a sluggishness and bashfulness, and a lack of virtuous boldness.[39]

---

39. Cf. *Betza* 25b; *Avoth* 5:20. Also see *Likutey Moharan* 22:4; 147, 271.

You are about to use your speech to overcome the great
battle against the evil within you. You are on the verge of
victory, and are about to break down walls with your words.
The gates are ready to fly open.

Will you then not speak because of mere bashfulness?
Will you hold back because of a minor barrier like this?

You are about to break down a wall. Will you be
discouraged by a spider web?

A person who has difficulties should spend two hours
each day in meditation. For one hour he should remain silent
and prepare himself to speak to God. Once his heart is
awakened, he can converse with God for the next hour.

Sichoth HaRan 232

36. Praying for All Things

You must pray for everyting. If your garment is torn, and
you have no money to replace it, pray to God for a new one.
Do this for all other needs as well. You will thus make it a
habit to pray for all your needs, large and small alike.

Of course, your main prayers must be for important
things. Pray that God help you in your devotion, and that you
be worthy of drawing close to Him. Still, you must also pray,
even for trivial things.

God may give you food, clothing, and everything else
you need, even if you do not ask for them. But then you are
like an animal. "God gives food to every living creature"
(Psalms 147:9)—even without being asked. He can give it to
you this way also. But if you do not obtain your necessities of
life through prayer, you receive them just like a beast. A
human being must receive all of life's necessities only
through prayer.

Rabbi Nathan relates:

Once I had a slight need for some insignificant thing.
When I mentioned it to the Rebbe, he said, "Pray to God for
it."

I was quite astonished to learn that one must pray to God even for such trivial things, especially in a case like this, where it did not even involve something that was really necessary.

Seeing my surprise, the Rebbe asked, "Is it beneath your dignity to pray to God for something minor?"

The main lesson is that one must pray for everything, no matter how trivial.

Sichoth HaRan 233

37. Avoiding Discouragement

Even if many days and years pass, and it seems that you have accomplished nothing with your words, do not abandon the practice. Every word makes an impression.

It is written, "Water wears away stone" (Job 14:10). It may seem that water dripping on a stone cannot make any impression. Still, as we can actually see, after many years, it can wear a hole in the stone.[40]

Your heart may be like stone, and it may seem that your words of prayer make no impression at all on it. Still, as the days and years pass, even a heart of stone can be penetrated.

Sichoth HaRan 234

38. Hodu

It is a Chasidic custom to recite *Hodu* (Psalm 107) to introduce the afternoon *Minchah* service before the Sabbath. When saying this Psalm, you can break your heart and express all your thoughts before God. This Psalm, which can be understood by anyone, speaks of the soul's troubles, and how one can cry out to God and be saved.

Sichoth HaRan 270

---

40. Cf. *Avoth DeRabbi Nathan* 6:2.

39. A Special Place

It is very good to have a special room set aside for Torah study and prayer. Such a room is especially beneficial for meditation and conversation with God.

Sichoth HaRan 274

It is very good even to sit in such a special room. Even if you just sit there and do nothing, the atmosphere itself is beneficial.

If you do not have a special room, you can still meditate and converse with God.

You can create your own special room under your tallith. Just drape your tallith over your eyes and converse with God as you desire.

You can also meditate in bed under the covers. This was the custom of King David, as He wrote, "Each night I meditate on my bed..." (Psalms 6:7).

You can also converse with God while sitting before an open book. Let others think that you are merely studying.

If you truly wish to meditate and express your thoughts to God, there are many ways to accomplish this. As we have discussed many times, it is the root and foundation of holiness and repentance, above all else. There are many ways of meditating, but the best way is to do so in a special, secluded room.

Sichoth HaRan 275

40. The Silent Scream

You can shout loudly in a "small still voice."[41] With this soundless "small still voice," you can scream without anyone else hearing you.

Anyone can do this. Just imagine the sound of such a scream in your mind. Depict the shout in your imagination

---

41. Cf. 1 Kings 19:12.

exactly as it would sound. Keep doing this until you are literally screaming with this soundless "small still voice."

When you depict this scream in your mind, the sound is actually ringing inside your brain. You can stand in a crowded room screaming in this manner, and no one will hear you.

Sometimes when you do this, some sound may escape your lips. The voice reverberating in your nerves may activate your vocal organs. They might then produce some sound, but it will be very faint.

It is much easier to shout this way without words. If you wish to express words, it is much more difficult to hold the voice in the mind, and not let any sound escape. Without words it is much easier.

Sichoth HaRan 16

41. Credit

A storekeeper will sell you things on a layaway plan, where they are paid for in advance.

Why not do the same with spiritual goods? Do a few good deeds, recite a few Psalms, learn some words of Torah, and let them be put aside and ready when you need them. You will then be able to make use of this merit at a later date. You will have prepaid with your good deeds.

Sichoth HaRan 271

42. Galbanum

Encourage yourself to pray. No matter who you are, you can encourage yourself and be stubborn, praying to God. If you are ever discouraged, meditate in the following manner:

I may be far from God because of my many sins. Let it be. If this is so, there can be no perfect prayer without me. The Talmud teaches that every prayer that does not include the sinners of Israel is not a true prayer.

Prayer is like an incense offering. However, the Torah requires that the incense contain galbanum (*chelbenah*, חלבנה),[42] even though galbanum has a vile odor by itself.

Thus, even if I consider myself a sinner, I am an essential ingredient to every worship service. No prayer can be perfect without me.

I, the sinner, must strengthen myself all the more to pray to God and trust that in His mercy He will accept my prayer. I am the perfection of the prayer—the galbanum in the incense.

Just as the vile-smelling galbanum is an essential ingredient of the sweet incense, so my tainted prayer is a vital ingredient of the prayers of all Israel. Without my prayer, all worship will be deficient, just like incense without galbanum.

Sichoth HaRan 295

The Rebbe once spoke about young married men who found their worship disturbed by the fact that they had not sanctified themselves properly in their marital relations. They felt tainted and found it difficult to pray.

The Rebbe warned us not to be discouraged because of this. He said, "The past is gone. When you pray, you must forget everything else. No matter what happened in the past, strengthen yourself now and pray properly."

He said that this is the meaning of Abba Binyamin's saying, "I am concerned ... that my prayer be close to my bed."[43] "Bed" here denotes marital relations.[44] Abba Binyamin said, "My prayer should be close to my bed. I should be able to pray even immediately after leaving my 'bed,' without being disturbed at all.

Sichoth HaRan 283

---

42. Exodus 30:34. Galbanum is the yellow-brown gum resin obtained from the Persian plant, *Ferula galbaniflua.* Alone it had a pungent, unpleasant odor (*Kerithoth* 6b). Others say that *chelbenah* was the gum of the common storax tree (Rambam on *Kerithoth* 1:1).
43. *Berakhoth* 5b.
44. Cf. *Kethuboth* 10b.

43. Paradise on Earth

It is a wonderful thing when a person is worthy of meditating regularly and in truth and expressing his thoughts properly before God. This is especially true if he is worthy of meditating in the fields and forests. With each step that such a person takes, he can experience a taste of Paradise on earth.

When a person returns from such meditation, he can often see the world in an entirely new light. It will appear that the world is entirely new, and that it is not the same world that he knew before.

Chayay Moharan 25b #4

44. Free Will

When the Rebbe told Rabbi Nathan about meditating and praying that God bring one closer to Him, Rabbi Nathan asked, "But doesn't this take away a person's free will?"

The Rebbe did not answer him directly, but merely said, "One must still pray." The Rebbe meant that even though this is difficult to explain, one must still pray for divine help in serving God. Actually, the same question can be asked regarding the formal prayers, where in the Amidah we ask God, "Bring us back, our Father, to Your Torah..."[45]

Shivechey Moharan 22b

45. A New Beginning

When meditating before God, it is good to say, "Today I am beginning to attach myself you You."

Whenever you meditate you should make a new beginning. Every continued practice depends strongly on its beginning. Even the philosophers say that no matter what one does, the beginning counts for half.

Therefore, no matter what, one should always make a new beginning. If one's previous devotion was good, now it

---

45. Cf. *Likutey Halakhoth, Choshen Mishpat, Pikadon 3.*

will be better. If it was not good, what better reason is there to make a new beginning?

Shivechey Moharan 23a #1

46. Childlike Simplicity

On Rosh HaShanah in Uman[46] shortly before his death, the Rebbe was visited by his grandson Yisrael, the son of his daughter Sarah.[47] At the time, the grandson was a very young child, around three or four years old. The Rebbe was then suffering from the tuberculosis that would take his life during the intermediate days (*chol ha-moed*) of Sukkoth.

The Rebbe said to his grandson Israel, "Pray to God for me so that I will become healthy again."

"Give me your pocket watch," replied the child, "and I will pray for you."

"He's becoming a professional wonder worker[48] already!" exclaimed the Rebbe jokingly. With that, the Rebbe gave the watch to the child.

The child then prayed, "God! God! Let grandpa get better!"

The people standing there began to chuckle. The Rebbe interrupted them and said, "This is how one must pray to God. How can one pray differently?"

He was teaching that the way to pray is with absolute simplicity, like a child before its parent, or like a person speaking to a friend.

Shivechey Moharan 23a #3

---

46. Uman is a city in the Ukraine where Rabbi Nachman spent his last few months. This is where he is buried.
47. Sarah was Rabbi Nachman's second child, born around 1790. Her son Yisrael was born in Kremenchug around January, 1807. The incident described here occurred on Rosh HaShanah 5571, which fell on September 29, 1810.
48. In Yiddish such a miracle worker is referred to as a *Guter Yid*, literally, "a good Jew."

47. Lord of the Universe

When you meditate, if you can only say the words, "Lord of the Universe" (*Ribono Shel Olam*, רבונו של עולם), it is also very good.[49]

The Rebbe once said that he can tell whether or not a person meditates.

Shivechey Moharan 23a #4

48. Various Lessons

The Rebbe once told one of his disciples to meditate once each day and once each night.

On another occasion, the Rebbe asked one of his followers if he was in the habit of sighing during his meditation. When the man answered that he did, the Rebbe asked him if he sighed from the depths of the heart. The Rebbe then said, "There are times that I sigh during my meditation. If my hand is then resting ont he table, it is some time before I have enough strength to lift it."

Once the Rebbe grasped Rabbi Sh'muel Isaac[50] by the garment over his chest and said, "Because of a small amount of blood like this, you can lose this world and the next!"

The Rebbe was speaking of the blood in the heart, which is said to be the seat of the Evil Urge. The Rebbe then continued, "Sigh and groan before God until you refine that blood, and subjugate the evil in it. You will then be on the same level as King David, who could say, 'My heart is hollow within me' (Psalms 109:22)."

Once the Rebbe spoke to Rabbi Yaakov Yosef[51] regarding serving God, as he often would. The Rebbe then told him the following parable:

49. In general, single word may be used; see above #2.
50. Rabbi Sh'muel Isaac of Dashev was one of Rabbi Nachman's earliest followers. He later became rabbi in Tchehrin. It is said that when he prayed, he appeared just like an angel.
51. Rabbi Yaakov Yosef's son married Rabbi Nachman's youngest daughter, Chayah.

A king once sent his son to distant places to learn wisdom. When the son returned home, he was well versed in all branches of wisdom. The king then told his son to take a large stone, the size of a millstone, and bring it up to the palace attic.

The son looked at the stone and realized that he would not be able to lift it. It was a huge, heavy boulder. He felt very bad because he would not be able to fulfill his father's request.

The king then explained his true intention to his son: "Did you really think that I wanted you to carry this huge boulder? Even with all your wisdom, you could not do it. My intention is that you take a hammer and break the boulder into small pieces. You will then be able to bring the entire boulder up into the attic."

The Rebbe explained that God wants us to "lift our hearts with our hands, to our Father in heaven" (Lamentations 3:41). But our hearts may be like huge heavy stones, which we cannot possibly lift, no matter what we do. What we must then do is take the hammer of words, and break and crumble our hearts of stone. Then we can lift them up to God. Understand this.

Once the Rebbe was speaking about how much one must engage in reciting Psalms and other prayers, as well as in meditation. Rabbi Yudel[52] asked him, "How does one get a heart?" He was asking how can one be worthy that his words should be with true awakening of the heart.

The Rebbe replied, "Do you think that you can attain true awakening of the heart from any *tzaddik*? The main thing is what you say with your mouth. You must recite many prayers and supplications with your mouth, and awareness of the heart will then come automatically.

Shivechey Moharan 23a #5

---

52. Rabbi Yudel of Dashev was among Rabbi Nachman's earliest disciples. Older than Rabbi Nachman, he had been a student of the famed Rabbi Pinchas of Koretz, and was a renowned Kabbalist in his own right.

When one of his great followers was young, the Rebbe told him that during his meditation, he should speak to each part of his body. He was to explain to each limb how all bodily desires are meaningless. The destiny of every man is death, when the body is brought to the grave. All parts of the body will then decay. The Rebbe told him to speak in this vein to each part of the body.

After trying this practice for a while, the follower complained to the Rebbe that his body was not listening at all to his arguments and words.

The Rebbe's reply was, "Remain strong in this practice. Do not abandon it. You will eventually see the result of these words."

The follower listened to the Rebbe's advice, and did as he had been instructed. Eventually, when he would speak to an individual part of his body, that limb would become totally paralyzed, without any power or feeling at all. This could actually be seen in the case of such external limbs as the fingers and toes. However, when he would speak to his vital internal orgains, such as the heart, he would have to speak very little, so that that organ not lose all vitality.

Once that follower was speaking with his friends and telling them that this physical world is nothing, and there is no point in that which pertains to the body. In the middle of speaking, he suddenly fainted. It was only with great effort that he was revived.

He then said that as a result of the Rebbe's advice, he had reached such a level that whenever he would speak about divine punishment or the final end of all the worldly, all parts of his body would feel it, even the small toe on his foot. They would all feel that they were already dead and buried, and beginning to decay. In order not to die, he would then have to strengthen himself and give his inner organs special encouragement.

The Rebbe told many people, whose bodies were gross and immersed in worldly desires, that they must speak to their bodies very much and convince them. They must tell their bodies about holiness and the purpose of life. One must also speak to himself very much and encourage him so that he will not give up completely.

Shivechey Moharan 23b #6, 7

Once, as if to complain, Rabbi Nathan quoted to the Rebbe the verse, "I am weary with my crying out. My throat is dry. My eyes fail while I wait for my God" (Psalms 69:4).

The Rebbe lifted his hands slightly and said very gently, "Therefore, what should be done?"

The Rebbe was saying that it is obviously forbidden to suspect God of not caring, and He is certainly just.

The Rebbe then said, "You must realize that when King David said in the Psalm, 'I am weary from crying out and my throat is dry,' he meant it literally. He had called out to God so much that he was weary and his throat had become dried out. But you still have your full strength..."

> *The following are lessons regarding prayer and meditation taken from* Likutey Etzoth.

49. The Weapon of Prayer

Your main weapon is prayer. You may have to fight many battles, both with the Evil Urge and with many other things that prevent you from serving God. With prayer you can conquer all.

If you wish to strive for holiness, you must engage in much prayer and in many conversations with God. These are your main weapons with which you can win the war.

You may pray and meditate for many days and years, and still feel that you are far from God. It may seem to you that God has hidden His face from you. Still, you should not mistakenly think that God does not listen to your prayers and meditation. You must believe that God listens and pay attention to every word of each prayer, so that not a single word is lost.

However, each word may only make a small impression on high when it comes to arousing the divine mercy. Therefore, it takes a long time until the structure is completed and you can enter it.

If you are not foolish, as the days and years pass, you will not become discouraged. Rather, you will become even stronger in your prayers. As a result of your many prayers, God will express His love. He will then turn to you, and enlighten you, fulfilling all your desires.

Sometimes you may be worthy of attaining some divine help, or some degree of closeness to God. Do not think that you were worthy of this because of your prayers and good deeds. All good deeds come from God. Our sages thus interpret God's words, "Who has given Me anything beforehand that I should repay him?" (Job 41:3) to indicate that God was saying, "Who can make Me a mezuzah before I give him a house?" and the like.[53] If not for God's mercy, one would drown in evil despite his prayers.

50. Life-Force

Life-force is obtained mainly through prayer, as it is written, "A prayer to God is my life" (Psalms 42:9). Through prayer, one also brings life-force to all three parts of creation: the lower world, the astronomical world, and the spiritual world. Through prayer, one motivates the power of the angels who direct the stars which oversee each blade of grass in this lower world, directing each one to grow. Our sages thus teach, "There is no blade of grass below that does not have a star and angel which strikes it and tells it to grow."[54]

Through prayer, as it were, a person also provides support to his heavenly Father (by fulfilling the purpose of creation). To the extent that one does this, God also provides him support and livelihood.

53. VaYikra Rabbah 27:2.
54. Bereshith Rabbah 10:7; Zohar 1:61a.

This is alluded to in the verse, "They kept His testimonies, and He gave them a *chok*" (Psalms 99:7). "They kept His testimonies" denotes prayer, through which we give testimony to God's unity. As a result, "He gave them a *chok*," where *chok* denotes food and livelihood.[55]

Through prayer, one can also find one's destined spouse.

However, when a person prays, extraneous thoughts come and the evil husks surround him, so that he remains in darkness and cannot concentrate on his prayers. The remedy for this is to be careful that the words leave his mouth with truth. Then, through the words that leave his mouth with truth, the person is provided with a passage through the darkness in which he is trapped, and he is then worthy of praying well.

Therefore, when one prays or meditates, even if it is impossible for him to say anything because of the great darkness and confusion that surrounds him from every side, he should still be careful to speak with truth, no matter what he says. Thus, for example, if he says, "God, help me!" he should say it with truth, meaning every word that he is saying.

Even if one cannot put any enthusiasm into his words, the least that he must do is truly mean the simple words that he is saying. Truth will then enlighten him, and he will be able, with God's help to pray and meditate properly.

Through this, one can rectify and sustain all the spiritual universes. He can also open doors to cause others to repent, and to help them escape from the traps in which they find themselves.

51. Praying for One's Needs

Make it a habit to pray for anything that you need at all times, whether livelihood, children, or healing for the sick. No matter what you need, your main plan of action should be

---

55. *Betza* 16a.

prayer. You should then believe in God, who is good to all, as it is written, "God is good to all..." (Psalms 145:9). God is good and helps, no matter what a person needs, whether healing, livelihood, or anything else.

If you believe this, your main effort will involve God. You will not seek other means, which often do not help in any case. Even if there are truly helpful means, they are not known, and usually are not available. Calling on God, however, is good and helpful for everything in the world. You can use this means at all times, since God is always available.

52. The Hidden Light

If you wish to experience the Hidden Light and gain an awareness of the mysteries of the Torah that will ultimately be revealed, you should engage in much meditation directed toward God. Judge everything you do to see if it is worthy and proper to act in such a manner before God who is constantly doing good for you. You thus sustain your words with judgment. You are bringing yourself to judgment, and you youself are the judge of all your deeds.

Through this, you can rid yourself of all fears. You will not be afraid of any official, lord, wild beast, robber, or anything else in the world. Your only fear will be an awe of God.

You will then be able to elevate fear to its root, which is Knowledge (Daath). You will be worthy of perfect knowledge, and thus know whom you must really fear. You will realize that the only One you must fear is God, where your fear is a deep awe of His majesty.

Through this, you will be worthy of understanding the revealed, non-mystical elements of the Torah. You will also be worthy of true humility. You will then be able to pray with literal self-sacrifice, annulling everything physical and all ego during prayer. You will thus be able to pray without any intent of gain, and will not think of the self at all. You will annul your physical being and your ego, and it will be just as if you do not exist.

Through this, you will then be worthy of comprehending the mysteries of the Torah. You will thus experience the Hidden Light, that will be revealed in the Ultimate Future. All this is attained through meditation.

Completed 17 Tammuz, 5740
July 1, 1980

INDEX

BIBLICAL QUOTATIONS

Selected titles available from the Breslov Research Institute

Advice
Aleph-Bet Book
Ayeh?
Azamra!
Breslov Haggadah
Breslov Music Book (Vols. 1-2)
Children's Treasury of Rebbe Nachman's Tales (7 volumes)
Crossing the Narrow Bridge
Esther
Garden of the Souls
Likutey Moharan (Vols. 1-5, 10)
Machiach: Who? What? Why? How? Where? When?
Mayim
Questions & Answers about Breslov
Rabbi Nachman's Stories
Rabbi Nachman's Tikkun (hard & soft cover)
Rabbi Nachman's Wisdom
Restore My Soul
Seven Pillars of Faith
Sweetest Hour
Tefilin
Through Fire and Water
Treasury of Unearned Gifts
Tsohar
Tzaddik
Uman! Uman! Rosh HaShanah!
Under the Table
Until The Mashiach
Wings of the Sun (Rebbe Nachman on Healing)

Also available: Music, Story and Home Study cassettes
books in French, Spanish and Russian;
You can visit our website on the INTERNET at:
http://www.breslov.org
e-mail - info@breslov.org

The Breslov Research Institute

The growing interest in Rebbe Nachman in all sectors of the Jewish world led to the establishment of the Breslov Research Institute in Jerusalem in 1979. Since then a team of scholars has been engaged in research into the texts and oral traditions of the Breslov movement. The purpose of the Institute is to publish authoritative translations, commentaries and general works on Breslov Chassidut in the major languages spoken by contemporary Jewish communities (English, French, Spanish and Russian).

The Breslov Research Institute also maintains a website on the INTERNET, featuring FAQs about Breslov, weekly Torah teachings, news and resources available around the world, study groups, #sessions, virtual library, links to other Breslov sites and....

Listed on the following page are offices of the Breslov Research Institute. We are not only honored to be able to supply Rebbe Nachman's teachings via book or tape, we are happy to answer your enquiries about Rebbe Nachman, Breslover Chassidim and Breslover Chassidut. Please direct your questions to any of our offices.

All our books involve extensive research and heavy production costs. This also applies to our tapes of the traditional songs and melodies of the Breslover Chassidim. All revenues from sales of our books and tapes are invested in further projects, but we still depend heavily on voluntary contributions. If you would like to share in making the heritage of Rebbe Nachman's teaching accessible to the modern world in English, French, Spanish, Russian and Hebrew, please make a donation in support of our work. (All contributions are tax deductible.)

The Breslov Research Institute also has several membership plans, to which you can subscribe for a year, for several years or for a lifetime. These plans range from a yearly membership which entitles you to all books and tapes published during that year (average yearly production is 4-6 units), to Club Members and Patrons, for full page dedications in our publications. Also available are various memoriams. Please write for details.

Internet Address: http//www.breslov.org
e-mail: info@breslov.org

ISRAEL:
Breslov Research Institute
POB 5370
Jerusalem, Israel 91053
Tel: (02) 582-4641
Fax: (02) 582-5542

USA:
Breslov Research Institute
POB 587
Monsey, NY 10952-0587
Tel: (914) 425-4258
Fax: (914) 425-3018
    1-800-33-BRESLOV

ENGLAND:
Breslov Charitable Foundation
3, Holden Road
Salford, M7 0NL
Manchester, England
Tel: (161) 792-6300

CANADA:
Breslov Research Institute
c/o Y. Levinson
119 Clanton Park Road
North York, Ontario M3H 2E4
Tel: (416) 636-4660

SOUTH AMERICA:
Breslov Research Institute
c/o G. Beilinson
Calle 69 #382
La Plata (1900)
Argentina
Tel: (54) 21-841-361
e-mail: Abi@cefex.satlink.net

SOUTH AFRICA:
Breslov Research Institute
c/o Baal Shem Tov Shul
POB 51501
Raedene 2124
Johannesburg, South Africa
Tel: (011) 640-3848
Fax: (011) 640-7129

Printed in Israel

זכרון נצח
לעילוי נשמות

הר״ר **משה מרדכי** בן הר״ר **שמעון נתן נטע** ז״ל
ר׳ **צבי דוד** ב״ר **יחזקאל** ז״ל
ר׳ **חיים אליהו** ב״ר **נתן** ז״ל
ר׳ **אליהו** ב״ר **יעקב** ז״ל
ר׳ **דוד** ב״ר **אברהם** ז״ל
ר׳ **שמואל** ב״ר **מרק** ז״ל
ר׳ **יעקב** ב״ר **מוריץ** ז״ל
ר׳ **דוד** ב״ר **מנחם מנדל** ז״ל
ר׳ **אריה לייב** ז״ל
ר׳ **שמעון ראובן** ז״ל

מרת **רות** בת ר׳ **אליעזר** ע״ה
מרת **מרים** בת ר׳ **צבי** ע״ה
מרת **בלומא** בת ר׳ **מרדכי** ע״ה
מרת **חוה** בת **פוליע** ע״ה
מרת **עטיל** ע״ה
מרת **אליס** ע״ה
מרת **בלומא** בת **לאה** ע״ה

ת.נ.צ.ב.ה.